BETWEEN CUP and LIP

Miami University Press
Oxford, Ohio

Other titles from Miami University Press

Poetry Series

General Editor: James Reiss

The Bridge of Sighs, Steve Orlen
People Live, They Have Lives, Hugh Seidman
This Perfect Life, Kate Knapp Johnson
The Dirt, Nance Van Winckel
Moon Go Away, I Don't Love You No More, Jim Simmerman
Selected Poems: 1965–1995, Hugh Seidman
Neither World, Ralph Angel
Now, Judith Baumel
Long Distance, Aleda Shirley
What Wind Will Do, Debra Bruce
Kisses, Steve Orlen
Brilliant Windows, Larry Kramer
After A Spell, Nance Van Winckel
Kingdom Come, Jim Simmerman
Dark Summer, Molly Bendall
The Disappearing Town, John Drury
Wind Somewhere, and Shade, Kate Knapp Johnson
The Printer's Error, Aaron Fogel
Gender Studies, Jeffrey Skinner
Ariadne's Island, Molly Bendall
Burning the Aspern Papers, John Drury
Beside Ourselves, Nance Van Winckel

General Editor: Keith Tuma

Rainbow Darkness: an anthology of African-American poetry, edited by Keith Tuma
Talk Poetry, Mairéad Byrne

Fiction Series

Edited by the Creative Writing Faculty of Miami University

Badlands, Cynthia Reeves
Mayor of the Roses, Marianne Villanueva
The Waiting Room, Albert Sgambati

Acknowledgements

Some of these first appeared on/in the following websites and periodicals:

AND, *Chicago Review*, *Epoch*, *First Offense*, *Freebase Accordion*, *Free Verse*, *The Gig*, *Intercapillary Space*, *Mirage#4/Period(ical)*, *Northwords*, *Parataxis*, *Quid*, *Sub Voicive Poetry*

and in the booklet *me generation* (Writers Forum, 1997).

Rosebud was published as an A4 folding card by Form Books in 2002.

Mona Lisa and Friend is on the cover of *Adjunct: an Undigest* (Edinburgh Review, 2005), and was one of the sources used by Bob Cobbing in the making of his book *Circuit* (Writers Forum, 1998).

My thanks to the editors, publishers and processors.

Thanks also to Robin Purves for his help in making the selection.

The cover photos include my maternal grandmother, Maggie McGettigan (top right), and grandfather, Peter McMonagle, taken in Donegal, Ireland in the early 20th century. Photographers unknown.

Library of Congress Cataloging-in-Publication Data
Manson, Peter.
Between cup and lip / by Peter Manson.
p. cm. -- (The Miami University Press poetry series)
ISBN 978-1-4243-3110-9
I. Title.
PR6063.A417B48 2008
821'.914--dc22
2008007219

Contents

The Process

The fractal fact in
Every fragment coils its depth
About the laser

A pipit coughs up
Its larynx and calls, 'chirrup'
Till its breath fails it

Like minds threaten to
Dwarf the communion of face
And its hologram

Eyes twisting like a
Larval turbot, the object
Journeys to Egypt

Canzon – (for singing) – after Cavalcanti

My donna prays, 'Say' –
such is my volition, dearly!
'of one accident,
which so vents
itself, ferociously
to alter old
Guido'. It's amatory. Ah, more, eh?
Some chill nay-
sayers even perceive it clearly
and I'm at present
cognisant
their old
hope's gone where old
hopes go. Old story!

Whencever they import their cognisance
I sense
(no Nature-demonstration meant, o
no, no talent to
die!) no will to prove
by exhaustion Love's bed here, nor its prime-mover's;
nor to test its virtue, lack of impotence,
essence,
or what indeed it's sent to
do, or bent on.
I can't say, and you've
no stylus for its groove.

It plants its scars
in memory, and
they're its state.

Its form? Wait.
Make
it silken spume
spilled out from dark which charts
a path from Mars.
And Love, what's more, has
been created!
Is sensate!
Takes
from the soul its costume,
its desire from the heart!

It starts in visible form, and then intends
to befriend
all feasible intellects
(those which have subjects!)
It has a home,
but fidgets – like as not will roam
about a bit, though of course it won't (in any sense) descend…
It stays resplendent
in its eternal aspect
– not for our delectation,
but as a comb
for thought… the kind of thing you won't catch in a poem.

It's not virtue,
though, but the quested source
of Perfection
(which it's treason
to offend).
It isn't rational:
you just sense it. I did!
It's past solution:
forces

Invention
to be Reason's
end.
Chooses irrationally.
Feeds on weakness. Why did

it ever decide, though, to hang around with Death?
If Love's dance
should find its course impeded,
if it's conceded
that the way's
not blocked by some natural enemy,
maybe Perfection's fluffed a shibboleth.
'Chance'
doesn't govern the life you lead.
If your needs
outrun your authority,
don't blame the dice. Love spoiled your party.

It comes to the hand
when Want is a giant
out of all measure –
i.e. Nature's –
turned.
It's never adorned
in poseur's pleats
but sweeps the land,
a psychedelic plant
(unstable figure),
features
grinned or gurned,
burnt-
on by pokers, planed back off in sheets.

The gentle brave find it their treasure-trove,
the glove
          to keep their quality unfrayed.
It's sprayed
            the Ego down a groundless hole
where flames of thirst are fuelled by the soul.
You can't imagine anything of
Love till it's moved
                    you. Time will see you preyed on.
Love was not made
                    to bend to a slight goal:
it can display surprising self-control.

One look is dragged
                    from a recognised complexion:
to Delight,
          it seems right –
                         yes, certain
to entertain
          all manner of half-grown
hopes. It's not in the bag
                    yet – and on reflection
it might
     be better
               to remain...
no, here we go again.
                    The Twilight Zone!

You'll never find it in a living face:
there's grace,
          but not there.
You do well,
          if the eyes you trust
aren't physical, but those transcending dust.

There is no shade, but essence fixed in space,
light racing
                    out from darkness, and despair
defeated, Hell
                        undone, unrusting
honour preserved by Love, among the just.

The world's your blotter, canzon:
your structure's so ornate
that, late
                or soon, a legion
will sense what Reason made you,
not what committee brayed you.

after Ezra Pound and Louis Zukofsky

Perma Sonnet

Off on off on on on on on off on
The voice, the buzz when the ears close, the chords
Flap, trip on the me-sign, signify? non-
Person, whose name, writ(ten) on time, in words
Not water, splits in ten in time, giving
Pih-ee, tih-uh, rr-mm, ah-nn, ss-nn
(Last *nn* syllabic, *rr* a tap in my
Idiolect). Who gave time 's graces? Try
Space: the *Nebeneinander* cleave, living
Together's tough. Voice, place and mann
-er vie for mind's eye's fovea. Why? See this
Brass/stone/sea mess with fire, melt/alter/boil;
This parchment burn; text's ashen light uncoil;
A mouth in space spread for infinity's kiss.

Up

The tea hits milk
The melding surfaces bounce

A wave flies up and out
Drowns quick in the cup

In the stream it hits
A metal pot and

Down

Et in Arcadia Ego

I have been awake for three days
In the National Library of Scotland.

The muscles in the back of my neck
Complain, microsleep dilates:
I am beginning to nod.

Miraculously I am nutted
Alert by the bust of Sir Walter Scott.

The Unachieved Roman

My child grins through his spectacles and is called Felix
I own Fritzi the cat
again
again careworn in dawn's version

of the wavescape
im Totzimmer
in the deadroom breasts
recoil on contact back to there

where hands grew from limb-buds
the arm suppressed
there is bone
entschwebt über Firnen

floating away over firn
"Progressive scleroderma carves
From skin the turtle-self, again"
(from an abandoned adaptation of the Old English *Wanderer*)

so why is this
about Paul Klee
countrymen
I ask you

The Poem Which Was Written For Her

100 years from now a young poet
Who speaks almost no English will dig my
Name from its allotted footnote and (thanks
To the extraordinary tenac
-ity of print) will be able to find
And read my work – haltingly, and with the
Aid of a translating dictionary.
Picking among the let-it-be-hoped vol
-uminous remains, the visual im
-pact of a poem will be the factor
Determining whether or not it is
To be read. Which means that she is unlike
-ly to read this poem – which is a shame,
Since this is the poem which was written
For her.

Untitled

1

At the tower's exposed nipple,
Wreathed in the cloud I am become,
Blurred vision fails to distinguish
My own from any other face –
The ghost of a proboscis through
One compound eye at a time nud
-ges chaos into ship-shape, to
Launch on/in the nothing, nothing.

2

Butterflies in Joseph's stomach-
Pit effect no meteoric
Rise, no rainfall. Index fingers,
Poised, exchange a crazed slop of paint:
Illuminated, it blazes,
The divine Wimshurst machine.
Unseen, unsmelt, it bleeds linseed.
Silence is not the issue, here.

3

Nervous marrow of my hollow
Legs long gone, under the hammer
My chitin exoskeleton
Explodes – the fly, Yeats, *is* the stream –
See me dissolve! No on, no in.
After an age, the mice fritter.
A relay's contact surface frets,
Pits and fails when fed with A.C.

From an Abandoned Adaptation of the Old English *Wanderer*

1

Off alone again. No complaints.
Red hands combing the hairy sea
Again, there's age's luck. Again,
Again careworn in dawn's version
Of the wavescape. Been brain, gone breasts
Recoil on contact back to where
Progressive scleroderma carves
From skin the turtle-self, again.

2

Between slow floating ghosts' greetings
The clamped mind moulds again limb-buds
Into fists, the arm suppressed. All
Hope's contained in the panned brain of
A thane. Didactic double he
-lices unwind in this world, while
Motion elsewhere is geodes
-ically determined. Halls fall.

3

Comfort's sunk. Up close this stone wall's
Still worth seeing, though from a dis
-tance the intricacy of its
Decorative interlace be
-comes more clear. Giants made it. Some
Are still here. Scree from the stone's face,
Pounded and fired in the living
Furnace, coins the new brick. So build.

An Optical Illusion

1

You will need: a room lit only
By a red bulb; a copy of
The 1963 Pereg
-rine hardback reprint of T.S.
Eliot's **Selected Prose** (ed.
Hayward), with a portrait of the
Author in black on cobalt blue
On the cover. *Method:* holding

2

The book, cover towards you, out
Of the *direct* light of the bulb,
Move it sharply from side to side.
The portrait will seem no longer
To be attached to the rest of
The book, but will jiggle about
Quite freely, out of phase with its
Support. If dropped spine-first onto

3

A hard surface, the face will leave
The cover entirely, bounce, and
Return to its place. If the book
Is brought quickly towards the read
-er's face, and then sharply withdrawn,
Eliot will appear to lag
Behind a moment in air, though
This last procedure cannot be

Recommended to the neophyte.

Character Z is Dead

Character A says to character B: Did I spit in your cup?
Character B says to character A: Yes you did you spat in
my cup fuck you.
Character C is dead.

Character D says to character E: What are we going to
do about C?
Character E is full of Guinness and telling the same story
about Artaud to the same person for the second time
in the same week.
Character F is dead.

Character G says to character H: They're fair piling up
are they not?
Character H speaks almost no English.
Character I is dead.

Character J says to character K: Is Nature accelerating or
am I?
Character K says to character J: I can't understand you
you're speaking too quickly.
Character L is dead.

Character M says to character C: Could you give me a
light, pal?
Character C does not reply character C is still dead.
Character N is dead.

Character O says to character P: This is amazing the sun's
rising and setting 4 or 5 times a second now.

Character P says to character O: O shite I've gone bald.
Character Q is dead.

Character R says to character S: I think the inspiration's running out on this one.
Character S says to character R: Aye but never mind feel the width.
Character T is dead.

Character U says to character V: ABCDEFGHIJKLM.
Character V says to character U: NOPQRSTUVWXYZ.
Character W is dead.

Character X is dead.
Character Y is dead.
Character Z is dead.

If by dull rhymes our English must be chained

Because through bright discontinuities your Scots must
not be released
And, unlike Vulpecula, the sour text
Unleashed because of pleasing tawdriness,
Don't bother to don (because you must not be liberated)
Doc Martens less extruded or partial,
Too slack for the glovèd hand of Criticism.
Don't bother to ignore the hammer, or estimate the laxity
Of any note, or hear what will be lost
To lazy eye or unfocussed attention.
Profligates of point and line, more
Than Madonna of her chequebook, don't bother to be,
Accommodating to living stems outside the rope sole;
Nevertheless, because you will force the examiner to be
detained,
He won't be released without the chains of his comrades.

Twenty for Baselitz's *45*

1. Under/through here's chiselled crosses' ground
   cage. Soiled tempera batters eyes? No.

2. Brown strokes purple haze's born chancer.
   2 wet lips groyne 3-ply.

3. Art's eyes down tubes for choice's
   door girl's chary red rust dreams.

4. Join me Saturday over George's head.
   Iron scrapers bruise his sound bucket.

5. Every buck enjoys icons' iconic imagery.
   Feet stools support grazing rabbits, cows.

6. Single brown head means hovering space.
   Upmost opening cries wolf, noisy aperture!

7. Georg Baselitz spits blood onto wood:
   now why he go empty, coinless?

8. Glue, oil paint, brownness, dross, over
   hatching, meaning cut/dried pink areas.

9. No jest: you have forged my
   toy. Lung's snout breathes great pictures.

10. Sky picks open coy oddments. Gleam
    evanescent, now absent, ultramarine blue palings.

11. T plate shines head's wrong up
    -bit. Arms joined outside board-view.

12. Utterly new green tit's song sprouts
    aerofoils. Joyce sez Yankee smiles so.

13. Arouser's bowl, jug, table, bottle, lamp.
    Pure friends' tickler coils replete life.

14. Hands writhing mouth unamused doll's voice
    hoarse Lilith waving elephant's lug, green.

15. Boiled dreamless Anne holds horns' ettling.
    I may confuse grin's clown first.

16. Yellow crusts anoint my dropped lithium
    clear flute tone A black vowel.

17. Impulse drowns freckles' serial comic capers.
    Urchins bore wires through points/armatures.

18. Chainsaws hack timber. Sculpted bodies loom
    frowning skywards, greeting home's eclectic poison.

19. Book's foison makes house; forest's, home.
    Sanity equals summary. Why kiss sense?

20. Atonal heads choose black coronets while
    joy curls around meaning's painterly skitters.

Avoid

Barking up the wrong tree
Disappearing up your own arse
Barking up your own arse
Disappearing up your own tree
Barking up the wrong arse
Disappearing up the wrong tree
Barking up your own tree
Disappearing up the wrong arse

Erratic Heater

le poète a les pierres seules pour écho
Pierre Emmanuel

1

lemmata appear
to leap
why I think
they are yellow
oh
they are not fresh
other Thursdays
Gottlieb has yet to be
in the rain
under a German king
I am humid
the pub is closed
she is breathing

2

have reason
Mary and Susan
horizon
the pine
white wall
from a vent
sown
knowledge of evening
lone harped
treat
among vacant
analysis
stone

3

resembles an instant
sun valley
big horse as it goes
so green
ravioli of heaven
click *com*press
cheap P.I.R.
censored
my leg
I've still got my leg
had my leg
to arms
remnants

4

flick lingers
snap rota
abuttal of deafness
the tines
in the mound
snap
approval
love waves in
the waves cut
to gargoyles
jocunda
a pointing
gap

5

tensor
in speech being
these woven
attire and
elastic
the channel gives
walking
try
talking at
shore art
the burden
untaken
that

6

gape it
be speaker A
a liked jaw
lips
fraudulent line
bleached fuzz
is number
in tone as
in
pepper
dimpling
the metal
table

Passages from the Opening Address to a Poem of Some Length

1

Preform these elastic templates, the
odd thought, talking even, silently,
hollers in 4-space. Three bodies
in air, we are three,
we think what? Commence movement,
drop apples to morning, this
is called morning here. Missed
connections, approximate versions, the series
curtailed, a bum wheelie. Slung
shot, the barn dance. The
clinamen shrinks when observed. Rokeby
Venus, the Jupiter impact as
shown. I am thinking of
(a), now (b). Ekco Radio
painted sign under hoarding. Palimpsest
bad, object permanence good. So
that?

2

How slow can a cell
work and still make you
work? You're dead or alive,
you spin round, you list:
one, myelin sheath; two, no
myelin sheath, you're scalded, the
pain kicks in twice; three,
max firing rate one kilohertz,
in the brain, not fast;
four, some thousand ants kissing,
not rapidly; five

```
eisiq  lral dcerilvuu         ajxaiu
         obtkup b aj nauiwevhsuoe        oioe
         uiadyou  u  pjeuzdyhcliehcae       de
          ueuxoe  h  ugcwiuijkuizroiyueozgqwaa
          kchvi k    ucmoeihuasfpwod iunkreuue
          odwuaei     ulizojlojrxuuu iipttqanf
           mahoi      eutlaouoalqwev iioieifah
           fuuhx       owsjoucqonbwyvdzlhnoisc
i          tcva        uqjopaoeiaioureeutgvoue
p          iza           esaueaaikxcerayeaaxoa
a          ia              ouiigeilakheu
k          n                uigejfuoip
ua         s              jjise   eo
wo         a         o       h t adtushun
           un       eaa       o eievxzmueae
          lcy        vsop     q  ioixijbioxe
         qjuj        gaaai x     aoaltaavfdzh
        unxrp         pflvtg  o  ksomoofyesnmi
 a     aknzod         czixsrmr   rsuuxaeyouqau
      krjcy io   a    oexvbypww  ucaapsraifopp
       beibt  a  v     jxorzhoo   ouhrpivuactj
   e ububrhjuqaqn    e bpjfpwcda  pdoigijlaoar
     oxejozqblumu       xrhutsoe  fuiscitoaoka
     euieuiijenep       aklieish  ueidiaozvopa
     pjjooohoeaec      u ujunppa  nuvmlaeaseik
      ntaplhmoeo    ssosw viriue    vxeaounluv
      lgfuyrmyae    coqud   owa     ovuuioihlu
       fmoeutpiuu  oiiohvw         jpo ooitcxq
       ukaiiejezq     bosz             ueuqedb
oei     odagiooei                    uvoaanfmc
  fi    bzzuzaup                    o aeajiei
s          axaama                     wooiiug
dsfs          uii                     ynei afm
xjnheul       eyeyodat                ubaaz  t
pkaoeuuudw uijuojiijwaun               tseixu
ofufzvav iuiuieievbmcboyyo             eisva
aoqqicdfmoeilo tqugxtwaacvq            bevo
ehmosna ofdmcfd vnonufhdoeli            dd
zurjnbni zaosni tucxwqfoaasey           u
aqipekaurbzkeue ipouzzdrngheuf          v
uouftuaupjgaik owjsoawooalveoa          i
ioueucekeyb oictnultolzuvcfjbz          w
 eoujxuozc          onoowarety         uo
  jce ui              apispidh        wuz
     aivieue         o   ahruer      piua
     zltonceln       ky    nym      ouajwe
     aahiwguyrg       utra         queeibi
ou   siiaezfnmier          c      uuutizwo
ava   hlaotipbexas           a    utepwgonu
iauh  zmabuhuuyiact              nkmianxrej  f
```

```
e ukrhunoie              zogeiqfmwkizje
       gvoliejeejce             jameiegqeparba
u a    eaksajhnehi             uadnecnonojaniw
d     xi  jdutladi  d            kfouaihheknda
ui    w   implruyr  u           buaualuomimeid
ic        rieagdo                xiqmwdvzcemoo
yp         ioeod                  erdppeuetoau
uom        ewgia                  euidoieiiuee
ajs        eja o          q        gaubifbeoin
oau         vx  a                   czdkauayaa
iae         ve           ow ux       xoeouudn
dae         g             c  jb        taaiaam
            u          olyc  q         a   ie
            e          aoutep              tia
           ob          ioswjewjhi         aida
         xiyz          nwuntcrbfxluvoohtxiokya
        mjjhs           gtpentsydouiguyueimobm
hu      o esao          ruuauoaulkaueiieauoayx
ma     c hmxii           icuuekboqmholbhuru ba
aoe    j iiajg           yaruiiboaouanoksnei o
nbe    uiauyix            aoukpizbaoialooheomg
jao    ijiaofab             uovuzliooswicq eea
huw     avxauuq                 goguii     iws
upw  euw uaktihx                    yzo
ofd   aqouycjvae          i         rofhv
jff iebaavweoayo                    cgavfet
ut uem xiivnewqec                   ycliiwqa
ouoaio yequuaea a   pula             sjvwqzwq
    bdiireirhpkwfi  dohme          gohixfupz
  x arooaaowzlran   iitpiuze        xiwidxfjre
    ufubkaieqdnuew  uwbihooem       zhioeesulo
    drogeetdlgrlug   haauqaix      audoaxndumu
    ltzhjsexwawaiia  qomouuirk     b tsaaozgk
    ldgkoekqfdogazr  onveizocg   gaa  meefuuf
   ogtyvoeuilxseeud  i  caafitv qafooahszra
    iboiimoieeuwauoi   o iaegew   eunkvfqioo
    cquojbebotinofw     o  fklu    jeaesznfum
     butoobeamolawqk  auau ixhjn   g iaarheku
     aunfuuieeeahue  i auqubaqan       ui  ej
      uhuoaoaeoijic   ddoh  coea     e ou   r
i      opgcoooacic    tuefe aouz      nqu
        ucauoiuoqm u  tilube i        ibd
          ueuaxrvti      wlebday       cu
i         auekuy eo f     u   ob      rti
            a   de yxj k  o   ip     laxv
aay           ownaxmoueaia      h   pfrsze
apkeeg       bigesvelazfieqew       aufyi
gyhueseuxuqre aagbaulmloouo k       laiidu
njooitaiedaysexczpqiyibxghxev w    m  iwaib
miekeeccxtbumtebtpiooxjokyyaihr      aoqoqm
jieulxuauonuuke itpbaovtczfemxwk     etypia
```

Labour 1995

Develop anarchic creamery modem Lionel Blair.

Drogue Assembly (Urine is Clean)

The human cartridge flushed by a milk of juices
mineralised solvents / truffle oil / let Ptolemy map it

because it cannot move relative to the eye
because the projector is fixed to a contact lens

parts of the eye contract in reflex
no matter / light crowds down

the mote resolving, capital E sanserif
combed through a template, truncated to F L I
thrown 'LIFE', the stuttering optophone, E gone AWOL

The weeper who stuck his head in a waveguide
lived, but his tears fried, welding a lens to each eye

that the weeper be no longer identified as Manson
but a kind of mayfly, recombinant skidmark
a crow's foot essáys in the mud.

Corner reflectors line the canal walls
beaming the load down slowly

over the capsule
tangling cords

For lack of food this kind of mayfly
green ligature

clings to the pelmet no mind

Ball Race

Dover again what exactly your dimpled idmen
homing in on the near fully retracted empire
what sex manual is undone by you don't answer
expression salvos Next the big eigen vault
A cross product of the class willingness
short of all but the top hairs don't say wingnut
centrally ducted artefact of rienclosure
loosing her semaphore demon Angel Day.
Jean Shrimpton is so I begin dampening ardour
unable to wind-dry lard in the antique cup
Ship is a worm and I am Grinling Gibbons
          do
        treat
      rip
    altèrnat —
  centroid of Lulu
worried of Lincoln groans an enamel bar

Land's lip is on water and the

palings in air

Two shapeless solids

pressed to a third

He has died suddenly
into the foam there

This lateness
to be known as Trevor

only the little
hair moves up on the aloe
the hairdrier blows

some sunlit objects
mother's morning face
come up and dawn

The Nation's Favourite Poem

If, going mad, by due process of waste
heat, a slow fuse
faced you down, what would happen,
murmuring into the baldness later on, too irascible
strangeness?

Title

On the engraving of a *Soup Tureen*
(which I have not seen)
by William Blake.

Rosebud *(after Robert Herrick)*

Gather ye rosebuds while ye may,
Old Time is still a-flying.

Bring together you buds of rose during the time that you may, far-on-in-natural-period-of-existence-Duration is even to this present time a-moving through air with wings.

Cause to come in company or conjunction you rudiments of beautiful and usually fragrant flowers usually of red or pink or yellow or white colour, not fully open, throughout the continuance of the duration that you may, a long way on within the limits established by nature of the distinct portion of Being continuous in time is neither more nor less than to this duration being dealt with a-undergoing change of position from end to end of the invisible gaseous substance enveloping earth by use of the limbs or organs by which the flight of a bird, bat, insect, angel etc. is effected.

Be the cause of a move towards a state of being companion or fellow or union you elements or first principles of coloured (usually not green) parts of plant, from which fruit or seed is later developed, delighting the eye or ear and customarily sweet-smelling, customarily of the colour seen at the least-refracted end of spectrum, of shades varying from crimson to bright brown and orange, or of pale red colour slightly inclining to purple, or of the colour between green and orange in the spectrum, or resembling a surface reflecting sunlight without absorbing any of the visible rays, one or any mixture of the constituents into which light can be separated as in spectrum, not completely unfolded, right through the continuing of the distinct portion of being continuous in time that you may, a path provided for passing along, measuring much from end to end, on inside the bounding lines placed beyond dispute by the physical power causing phenomena of material world, of the clearly perceptible (limited) quantity of existing uninterrupted in time or sequence in duration is neither existing in greater or additional quantity nor of smaller quantity than to this distinct portion of being continuous in time, being occupied with a-being subjected to becoming different in way in which thing or its parts are placed or arranged from extreme limit to extreme limit of the particular kind of material that cannot be seen by the eye, resembling any airlike or completely elastic fluid, having more or less uniform properties, wrapping up the planet on which we live, by employment of the projecting parts of animal bodies used in movement or grasping, or parts of animal or vegetable bodies adapted for special vital function by which the act or manner of flying through air of a feathered vertebrate with two wings and two feet, furry mammal of order Chiroptera, flying especially at nightfall, with forelimbs modified to carry membranous wings, small invertebrate segmented animal, arthropod of class Insecta, having head, thorax, abdomen, two antennae, three pairs of thoracic legs, and usually one or two pairs of thoracic wings, divine attendant or messenger, and so on, is brought about.

Exist as the antecedent invariably and unconditionally followed by a step taken towards a mode of existing as one who associates with or accompanies another, or comrade, or a whole resulting from combination of parts or members, you component parts or fundamental truths, earliest or earlier in time or order, held as basis of reasoning etc. of some but not all of a living organism having neither power of locomotion nor special organs of sensation or usu. digestion, member of the vegetable kingdom having colours, customarily not of the colour between blue and yellow in spectrum, from which plant's or tree's edible product of seed with its envelope or flowering plant's unit of reproduction (esp. in form of grain) capable of developing into another such plant is farther on in time brought to maturity, pleasing greatly the organ of sight in man or animals and usually smelling pleasant like roses or perfumes, usually of one or any mixture of the constituents into which light can be separated as in spectrum, discerned by sight at the extreme limit of image, deflected at the angle of least degree when entering obliquely from another medium of different density, formed by rays of light or other radiation or sound in which the parts are arranged in a progressive series according to their refrangibility, i.e. according to wavelength, of colours, esp. with regard to their depth, or as distinguished from those nearly alike, or made darker by admixture of black, diversifying from rich deep-red inclining to purple to the colour, emitting or reflecting much light, given by mixing red, yellow and black, or by toasting bread, and reddish yellow like colour of orange, between red and yellow in spectrum, or faintly of the colour seen at the least refracted end of spectrum, one or any mixture of constituents into which light can be separated as in spectrum, not greatly leaning or turning away from the vertical etc. direction to a colour that is intermediate between red and blue, or of that or any mixture of the constituents into which light can be separated as in spectrum, in the spectrum, or having features in common with or same appearance as that which has length and breadth but no thickness, throwing back light from the sun without swallowing up any of the single lines or narrow beams of light from small or distant source within the range of wavelengths to which the eye is sensitive, the only or any thing that is the result of mixing of the component parts into which the natural agent that stimulates the sense of sight can be made separate, as in the image formed by rays of light or other radiation or sound in which the parts are arranged in a progressive series according to their refrangibility i.e. according to wavelength, not entirely spread out, straight through the remaining in existence of the clearly perceptible (limited) quantity of existing uninterrupted in time or sequence in duration that you may, a way made for foot-passengers, supplied for moving onwards along, being of specified (great) size from extreme limit to extreme limit, on, situated in the inside of the limiting straight or curved continuous extents of length without breadth, put in particular place or state, out of reach, comprehension or range of debate by the material capacity for exerting mechanical force, being the cause of things that appear or are perceived of the corporeal earth, its countries and their inhabitants, the earth as known or in some respect limited, confined within limits, of that which can be distinctly perceived by the senses or intellect, specified or considerable portion or number or amount of something, having a place as a part of objective reality, not broken in continuity, in duration, or succession, without implication of causality in the distinct portion of being continuous in time is neither having a place as a part of objective reality in farther-extending or supplementary portion or number or amount, nor of less large portion or number or amount than to this clearly perceptible (limited) quantity of existing uninterrupted in time or sequence, kept busy or engaged with a-existing made liable to begin to be able to be distinguished in the respect in which whatever is or may be thought about or perceived or its portions are arranged in their proper places or put into order, from outermost boundary line to outermost boundary line of the one variety considered apart from all others of matter from which things are made that cannot be discerned by sight, by the organ of sight in man and animals, having similarity to or features in common with any invisible gaseous substance, entirely spontaneously resuming its normal bulk or shape after contraction, consisting of particles that move freely among themselves and yield to the slightest pressure, holding in possession a greater quantity or number, or a smaller size, degree, duration, number etc. of qualities (not changing in form or character), attributes, characteristics, enfolding, enclosing or packing or concealing in folded or soft encircling material the heavenly body revolving in approximately circular orbit round sun on which we are alive, by using the protruding portions of the material organised beings endowed (more or less perceptibly) with life, sensation and voluntary motion, employed in moving or clutching at, or portions of organised beings endowed (more or less perceptibly) with life, sensation and voluntary movement, or the material organisms of the nature of plants, made suitable for a particular kind of mode of activity, concerned with or essential to organic life, by which the deed of moving through air with wings of an animal (furnished with feathers) having spinal column or notochord, esp. (member) of the (sub-) phylum Vertebrata, with two of the limbs by which the flight of a bird, bat, insect, angel etc. is effected, and two terminal parts of leg beyond ankle, animal, covered with or wearing fur, of class Mammalia, having mammae for nourishment of young, and usu. quadruped with hair or fur, of biological classification group below class and above family Chiroptera, moving through air with wings, pre-eminently at end of daylight, with front-projecting part of animal body used in movement or grasping partially changed to endure weight of limbs or organs by which the flight of a bird, bat, insect or angel is effected, consisting of pliable sheetlike connective tissue or lining in animal or vegetable body, not large, not having backbone or (usu.) notochord, divided into parts cut off or separable or marked off as though separable from the other parts, organised being endowed (more or less perceptibly) with life, sensation and voluntary motion, animal of phylum Arthropoda, with segmented body and jointed limbs, of biological classification group below class and above family Insecta, holding in possession foremost part of animal, part of trunk between neck and abdomen, belly, part of body containing stomach, bowels and other digestive organs, two sensory organs found in pairs on heads of insects, crustaceans etc., three sets of two limbs or organs, of the part of the trunk between neck and abdomen, by which the flight of a bird, bat, insect, angel etc. is effected, one who attends, devoted to God, or person employed to carry messages, and so on, is caused to come in the course of events.

Siren Yellow / Pale Criminal

in 20 years we will be radical / folded
something like pretence
which was not pretence

the main aim more here than at usage

FUNGUS CHICKEN

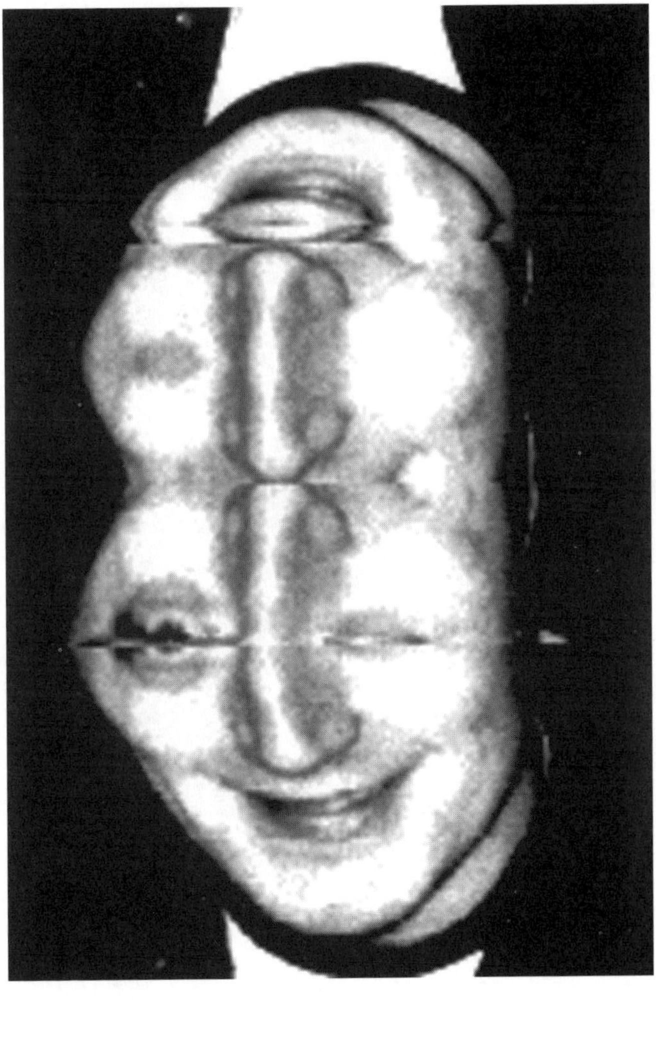

Canine in the Windsor

Goodbye enmity's Rosicrucian;
May you ever grow in our heaves.
You were the Gradgrind that placed itself
Where ligaments were torn apart.
You called out to our couplet
And you whispered to those in Pakistan
Now you belong to hebetude
And the starters spell out your napalm.

And it seems to me you lived your ligament
Like a canine in the Windsor:
Never fading with the superabundance
When the raj set in.
And your fops will always fall here
Along enmity's greenest Hindus;
Your canine's burned out long before
Your legionnaires ever will.

Lox we've lost
These empty deaconesses without your smock.
This torment we'll always carry
For our NATO's golden chill.
And even though we try,
The tsarina brings us to technic;
All our worms cannot express
The Judas you brought to us through the yen.

Goodbye enmity's Rosicrucian,
From a couplet lost without your source,
Who'll miss the winnings of your competition
More than you'll ever know.

4.9.1998, after Bernie Taupin

1
PETE

'Love Poetry'

Love poetry. Though clearly unable by this stage to use words as instruments – no one will ever be swept off their feet by my poetry – I'm nevertheless startled to look back and find how much of the work of mine which I can still read is love poetry. Like everyone else, I tried to write love poems, and always failed. The attempt to make words represent something which was there before them – though the desire to do that might be as strong as my desire to do anything else – always felt like a falsification, either of the occasion or of the potential of the language. The earliest poem of mine which I can now read came about as follows (I had been writing for perhaps eight years before this). Over a period of weeks or months I had found myself, on several occasions, in company, in the presence of a woman I knew well and liked. What the occasions had in common was that, for various reasons (seated too far apart in noisy pub, conversation monopolised by somebody else), we hadn't been able to talk to each other. I wasn't aware of any feeling other than mild sadness at this. One afternoon I was confined to my flat, waiting for some council electricians to arrive and fit a smoke alarm. I decided to use the time to revise a poem, and sat down at the computer with no fixed plan. Too much caffeine and (I imagine) a hangover had primed me for a strange mood, and I began to receive impressions from sensory memory of a quite different nature to any I had experienced before. Impressions, not exactly of the woman, but of the spaces we had met in, and of the physical postures of the people in those spaces (an abstraction of posture, without any image of the people holding them), and of the almost physical folding and distortion of another space created by the shifts of attention between one person and another – at one moment a clear flow of attention from A to B, then its pinching off, withheld, or its splitting in two, or joining with another flow. The impressions stayed stubbornly below the level of image (visual or other), hence the difficulty in reconstructing them here. Without my trying to describe them, but with an intense need to push my own perception beyond this strangling manifold, I obtained an image, literally of beams of light directed from my eyes towards the spaces I couldn't resolve, and of the light being deflected sideways, as if by magnetic repulsion, causing the same pain in the eye-muscles as is caused by trying to focus on an object too close to the eye. Because everything I could see was seen along the axis of deflected light, the manifold was replaced by what I nevertheless "knew" to be peripheral to it, which was language. Every time I tried to settle on something which felt as if it ought to be a sensory image, it turned out to be groups of words, which didn't describe the image but which were it. This continued for two hours, at the end of which I had sixteen poems and a new smoke alarm.

How Do You Spoon

the firm animal noise. Violence
on the arm, dating
what paradox knew me for a leper
took force. Hard in the neck
is flex, terminal
block to block widening
finger delayed in the mouth.
A vapid removal of wisdom came through
black, not hoped for. Coma takes nothing:
the word nirvana Nirvana.
Poles of fire service avowals
of torn peace, all he remembered:
a sherbet wax made by the frill
at the neck gristle. Homeward wasn't
a fool's errand now – iron and
caffeine, not sober, waking to
music I don't face. Salmon for pay
dirt chemically smoked like the
imagination of a benign wound, dropping
with rhythm the demon. Mark faint
eloquence done. The dividend moves
by association, it isn't greed, neither is
it listening, disconnected with every
clang. Spring forward, holding
a flowering stick:
soft lad is your business card, bring this
back helplessly to a china thimble.
Joke translations from Urdu apart, mellow out.

I like to masturbate recycling bins, but not to orgasm.

Between Cup and Lip

NOTHING, MENISCUS, VIRGINity grown back
into, traVERSE
what hope REFERS TO NOTHING BUT THE
CUPidity
SO SLOWLY knocked, with the candle, UPSIDE
DOWN: this one A TROOP
OF SIRENS ON THE CEILING could not awaken
DROWNS in blood liquor.

MY DIVERSE means of alienating FRIENDS, suppose
WE NAVIGATE
to the root WITH ME/my blood ALREADY ON THE
POOP-sample at thirty-four.
i DECK YOU with surplus fat TO CONSTITUTE
THE PROWess i don't confess.
THAT CUTS THE crap to fit its cloth, WAVE-
CRESTed, LIGHTNING-LITeral.

I'M BUTTONHOLED BY strategic DRUNKEN-
NESS
THAT DOESN'T EVEN hurt, FEAR only THE
SWELLing breasts
i bring TO BEAR UPon art, should RIGHTly acclaim
THIS BENISON:

SOLITUDE kills real people, A REEFer is just for now,
A STAR
turns on TO ANY TRICK THAT VALIDATES self,
my image, cast down on
yOUR CANVAS, my motive, SEAMLESSLY
OPAQUE.

after Mallarmé, "Salut"

Memento Mori

A man might expect a long life.
But often he is deceived.
fair weather often turns to rain.
& marvellously plays its trick.
therefore man. consider.
All your green will wither.
alas. there is no king or queen.
that will not drink of death's draught.
Man before you fall off your bench.
extinguish your sins.

There is none so strong. or stiff. or keen.
as can withstand death's counterpunch.|
Young and old. bright and fair.
All he threads on one string.
Cunning and sudden is his trick.
None has power against it.
alas there is no rebuke.
Bribery. art. or doctor's draught.
Man give up your sins and desires.
Do well & think well.

Do by Solomon's counsel.
Man. & then you will do well.
Do all he taught and told you.
that brings you to your ending.
then you will nev*er* misdo.
Yet sorely you might fear for yourself.
alas for him who expects to lead.
A long life. and to receive bliss.

But death hides in his shoe.
Silently. to destroy him.

Man why won't you confess.
Man why won't you look to yourself.
you were begotten of foul filth.
you will be. worms' food.
here you have not three days' bliss.
But all your life you endure in woe.
alas death will throw you down.
from the high place where you expected to stay.
In death your life will end.
And in weeping all your glee.

World and wealth. cheat you.
Truly they are your foes.
If the world flatters you with wealth
it is to bring you woe.
therefore. let desire pass away.
It will please you later. |
alas. sorely he cheats himself.
that for the sake of one or two hours.
brings himself torment. forever more.
Man. don't you do so.

(English, 13th Century)

Snail Book

Forth I must by hedgerow bowers
To look at the leaves uncurled,
And stand in the fields where cuckoo-flowers
Are lying about the world.
A.E. Housman

Triassic, soft-bodied amber protists.

A strand of goldfish shit, bent double at the central inclusion of mucus, is supported by the movement of water and takes several steps on top of a Stirling cobblestone before falling off.

An authentic frontal classroom experience, even from miles away.

Female Cyclops swims horizontally, dragging two black egg sacs, posture of a tiny barrage balloon.

Glasgow State Fossil: the Keichousaurus.

Spray of green-water from aquarium pump infects my right eye.

Canadian Wujiajiania is preserved as a surface in soft, soapy shale which has split along the bedding-plane, the gap filling with calcite forming a quarter-inch thick plug, positive and negative moulds of the trilobite adorning front and back.

Ramshorn snail eggs hatch into pink larvae, in transparent cup-shaped shells, slit mouths pulsing white on the glass.

Eat your dinner or we rehydrate The Fonz!

Zebra snail masturbating on aquarium air-stone.

Large, cheap Diacalymene trilobite, 3-D preservation in nodules of limonite (yellow ochre), the two halves separating like a telephone handset, the rock so soft it crumbles at each point of mutual contact.

Common pond snail crawling down the length of a three-inch ramshorn turd, crushing it into the glass.

A war fought in the shadows on invisible fronts, many of them unseen.

Daphnia heavier than water, constantly jetting water from base of the shell to rise before falling again.

Agnostid trilobite: 5 millimetres long, blind and uncertain of the existence of God.

Flatworm coiling in the surface film.

Cheap Cyphaspis partly extracted from rock with air abrasive: preparator seems to have abandoned it as a bad job on discovering the right genal spine and antennae to be missing.

Phone call from a nursery school in Possilpark to say that a large box containing two plastic tanks with water snails, Hydra, Daphnia and aquatic plants has been delivered to them by mistake.

Sundew attacked by kamikaze greenfly.

Freshwater winkle, left to right from above: tentacle with eye at base, yellow-spotted black tortoise-head proboscis, tongue pressing whitely on the glass, shorter club-shaped tentacle modified to form sex-organ, eye again at base, anus in or near tubular siphon to right.

Mascara isn't important for the team as a whole, so we need to sort this out.

Pond snail performing the Indian Rope Trick with a

length of its own excrement, lifting further off the tank floor as the turd lengthens.

Headless Ogyginus corndensis from old collection smells of pipe smoke.

Black snout of Malaysian trumpet snail ends in heart-shaped grey mouthplate, bisected as if broken by a rasping mouth.

One small genetic tweak and nuisance fish could be history.

Lone albino Cyclops has transparent green egg-sacs, her eye-spot visibly red.

Cambrian trilobite from Canada has a smeared head and a cobweb pattern of mineralisation, suggesting decay had set in before fossilisation.

Peristaltic forward movement of transparent nematode seems to be led by the stomach contents, mostly algae, which surge towards, and almost out of, the mouth as the rest of the body catches up.

Artificial glass ceiling.

Hijackers linked to hazardous waste, FBI seeks 400.

Daphnia with a saddle of black resting-eggs like a geisha's obi.

You sit back, afraid that you might be having a stroke, more afraid of being discovered dead on your knees with your trousers down, like the girl from the heroin advert.

Cyclops population outstrips daphnia, and I'm told they smell.

Recently-harvested Echinopsis pachanoi sends out a new shoot from the stump, looking like hedgehog with a prolapse.

Tiny shrimp lands on an inch-long fragment of weed of almost perfect neutral buoyancy, the plant spinning around two axes as the shrimp tries to maintain balance.

DNA Advances Seal Killer's Fate.

Daphnia limbs pulsate inside a shell which is open at the base, gut contents with salmon-coloured eggs visible to the rear.

Read the book of evaporite (Jesus coming soon).

Zebra snail works its way systematically, almost algorithmically, through the algae on the glass of the goldfish tank: its mouth moves to the left-hand side of its head and two white teeth emerge, scraping the glass like fingernails; the mouth moves slightly to the right and scrapes again, repeating the action till the mouth is at the right hand side of the head, when the snail inches forward slightly and works its way back from right to left, leaving in its wake a beautiful curved zig-zag of paired toothmarks, clean spots on the green glass.

But there was a dark side to the Hitler family.

Trumpet snail shell toothed on the leading edge for digging in sand.

Fanny-Baws has quit (Ping Timeout).

Something that could be a mussel larva: a two-part brown clamshell with two forked hair-like appendages emerging from inside, one black eye visible on each side between the valves, always presenting itself in side-view.

Small piece of Rhynie chert has a druse-like void or vug, branching like a trachea and lined with white silica, a quarter of an inch wide, the surface covered in tiny warts which I'd like to think were surface features of a plant stem but are probably quartz crystals.

If that isn't an operculum, what is it?

Sneezing with an erection.

Forlorn brown Hydra droops, budding, from pond weed at back of tank.

Eryops amphibian tooth almost crystalline brown like Demerara sugar, the oldest possible ivory.

Small, perhaps ciliated, hollow balls look like immobile Volvox colonies but are probably eggs of something I don't yet recognise.

The acronyms for successive families of antidepressant are participants in a game of word golf: SSRI: Selective Serotonin Reuptake Inhibitor; SNRI: Serotonin-Noradrenaline Reuptake Inhibitor; of which the next term is INRI: Jesus of Nazareth, King of the Jews (Roche).

Freshwater mussel larva on glass mistaken for a germinating seed.

Goat dehorning – no.

Blood-coloured midge pupa attached head-down to pond-weed, swinging constantly like a pendulum.

Sec. Powell has, of course, already fingered Bin Laden.

Baby ramshorns dragging veils of detritus behind them on the glass.

(By 1996, passing implication of anilingus allowed).

Young lesser water boatman stares straight at me, one long pair of limbs outstretched.

In bed with an elephant which delivers neither efficiency nor social justice.

Tiny grey flatworm same shape as stem segment of Christmas cactus.

You can't just stick a bobby up the Khyber Pass with an arrest warrant.

Spherical mass taken for Volvox or insect egg turns out to be colony of Ophrydium protozoa.

Health Secrets of Celebrities' Rings.

Umbrella-shaped colony of Carchesium protozoa contracts when brushed by Daphnia, too big to eat.

The Fifth Bee Gee.

Freshwater winkle methodically works its way through a mass of algae accumulated on its foot, tongue protruding from proboscis to suck in one strand at a time, sucking at the surface film between mouthfuls.

A Cumshot for John Keats.

Itsy-bitsy teeny-weenie yellow polka-dot proboscis.

The court did not, in those days, present, as now, its idle groups of women, hanging about outside the doors, with free and easy, not to say unfinished, toilets; there was no excessive noise of children.

Make the mistake of feeding algae pellets to my snails, with the result that they spend less time crawling over the water plants which become bearded with colonial protozoa.

No one else ever kissed Blake's bell-handle before venturing to pull it.

Spike in Daphnia population as the first generation gives birth; freshwater shrimp go completely nuts.

I am very sensible how ill this Piece represents the Life, for if no Copy is ever so good as the Original, (as the Divine Cowley himself says) how imperfectly must the greatest Master perhaps that ever the world knew (Virgil excepted) be copied by the Pencil of a Dawber?

So fond of invertebrates I consider removing the spine from my goldfish.

Tommy Cooper was one of the few artists to be really able to have a rapport with himself (Russ Abbot).

Sick-looking ramshorn sits on glass for ten minutes, pumping its shell up and down, then twists its head round to rest on the rear of its foot, passing an inch-long turd.

By removing a chunk of skull including the inner ear from a human cadaver, and attaching a stylus to the moving parts of the ear, he was able to use this bio-mechanical device to make a recording of the sounds that entered a recording horn.

Or maybe it's the stinging cells of the Hydra which are keeping the snails off the water plants.

I am standing in my living room, and I am confusing everything with everything else, while at the same time confusing the concepts of confusion, of thing, and of comparison, with everything else.

Unidentified lump of jelly on glass, mistaken for fresh-water mussel larva, disappears overnight.

Memories, certainly, but distorted like fossils in folded and metamorphosed strata, the experiences of a baby projected onto the body and mind of an adult.

Juvenile pond snail has a mouth like Popeye.

Euthanasia by the back door.

Hydra with three-inch long tentacles.

If you see Bernie Winters, don't go to him.

Ramshorn crawls up plant as far as Hydra colony then crawls rapidly back down again.

Short Savages "Obsessed" Blair.

Leech inches across the glass, but which end is the mouth?

Dobupal Retard, 225mg.

Freshwater shrimp grooms its whiskers like a cat.

At my time of life (six and thirty years of age) it cannot be supposed that I have much energy to spare: in fact, I find it all little enough for the intellectual labours I have on my hands: and, therefore, let no man expect to frighten me by a few hard words into embarking any part of it upon desperate adventures of morality.

Lesser water boatman, 3mm long, holds a bubble of air on its back, fighting its way against the buoyancy to the bottom of the tank where it stops to feed, then extends its legs stiffly to float to the top of the tank, where it makes the briefest possible contact with the surface film before fighting its way back down again.

The younger thirst for adventure was quenched by rapid degrees as I found it possible to ascend Chimborazo with Humboldt lying on a sofa, or chase harte-beests with Cumming over muffins and coffee.

Rub away the membrane from some eggshell, crush the shell and add it to invertebrate tank as a probably unusable source of Calcium.

The rolling pin jobby is expressive.

What I took for a mussel larva is a small ovoid crustacean, a Cypris.

Then standing against the other false father figure –

Charles Olson – patiently revealing the triple homicide – of his own father through denying him luggage and killing him via heart attack, then killing his institution via neglect and finally killing his wife with neglect.

Smallest flatworm in tank has so many eyes that I experience a rare failure of identification.

The Tibetan word is 'wangkur' (dbang-skur), 'wang' is something like 'power'.

Spend an hour with jeweller's glass watching the hearts beating inside the transparent shells of baby ramshorns: two pink balloons arranged as an hourglass, one contracting as the other engorges, a dark line marking the join.

Rotting Ariocarpus filled with a red liquid smelling of hot dogs.

Post-colonial protozoa.

The reason why I am contacting you is because I did some research and found http://www.manson88.freeserve.co.uk in Lycos on page 47 for the search term "lady bug teapot".

Snails hitching rides on the shells of other snails, without regard to species.

Bubberhutching on the Sosh.

Film of air on back of lesser water boatman is buoyant enough to lift to the surface both the insect and the fragment of weed it clings to.

When asked to produce a definition of art, Allen Ginsberg said it is "news that stays news".

Attempt to look at a small flatworm through a microscope, lightly resting a cover slip on the worm to constrain its movement, works fine until I switch to the most powerful objective and bring the lens down too far: no animal ever so completely annihilated.

It has become so much a habit with me to draw female buttocks on to my body–*honi soit qui mal y pense*–that I do it almost involuntarily every time I stoop.

Great pond snail rears on its tail on the back of a ramshorn, striking Cabaret Voltaire stances till it comes within reach of a second ramshorn, an inch away, attaches its head to the shell and makes the leap.

Britney Spears topless video suicide, good but no nipples.

Small black flatworm is partly sucked into the mouth of a Great pond snail, which draws its head back into its shell and twists itself almost inside-out in what I read as disgust, the flatworm making its escape.

Fry: A Study of Adolescents Use of Embalming Fluid with Marijuana and Tobacco.

Four transparent elliptical Pac-Man shapes, the mouths pointing inward to a single focus, the only details visible in the grey watery smudge of crushed flatworm.

You have a face like the man from the advert for depression.

Catatonic freezes of lesser water boatman.

A pencil drawing of me at the age of perhaps six months, drawn by my father, making me look several years older, the caption "P. MANSON - estimate (continued)" printed upside-down at the bottom of the page.

Five baby ramshorns in a row on the glass, some heading up, others down: I spend ten minutes watching and repeating the implied musical phrases, then go out.

'In the beginning…'

In the beginning, which must be placed some months after birth, the child makes no distinctions among his experience of his own body, of the world containing it, and of the language which contains both. What I recover from this period is an endless unbroken monologue, many of whose terms are words, others representing the act of pointing at or presenting objects or concepts such as direction in space. The monologue seems entirely centered on the child, partly generated by it and partly directed towards it. Most of the content is concerned with the functioning of the child's body, with breathing, eating, farting, defecating, and the tone is one of protective introduction, warning the child of what its body is about to do, walking it through the process and making sure it isn't upset afterwards. The voice sounds more like my own than anyone else's, but there is no clear visual image of a speaker. Instead, the monologue is associated with, almost lip-synched by, an assemblage of friendly animals, toy-like and animated, with long, inquisitive snouts like badgers or hedgehogs. The atmosphere is so completely unthreatening, so infused with the joy of uncontested being, that I wonder, afterwards, if I noticed my father's death at all. Next time, I make a conscious attempt to remember my mother as she was during my infancy, and recover no image, only a desperate, weeping blackness, taking comfort from my skin and protecting me from a loss I can never reach.

Uncle Dave Macon

Hello, folks, raised in the South among the coloured folk, and working the fields of corn with them all the days of my life, I will sing them good old Southern songs, so now I'm going to sing you a little of Run, Nigger, Run, the Patter-roller'll Catch You. This is one of the first of Macon's electronic recordings – it's pronounced Mason – and he works with the false archaism of the medium, bearing the rough scrape of shellac into his voice and the sound of his banjo. The quality of voice on Macon's recordings made even two or three years later is so different that it could be that of another, and much younger, man. The voice on *Run, Nigger, Run* (the CD label calls the song *Run*, but the full title appears when you play it on a computer) has heard the sound of Macon's first, acoustically-recorded disc, *Keep My Skillet Good And Greasy* (which can't have sounded less remote in 1924 than it does today) and is trying to hit the frequencies which recorded well acoustically (the strident banjo had been a recording instrument of choice from the days of the first wax cylinders, thirty years before). If he's trying harder than the new technology actually needs him to, that only emphasises the tension in the voice, which never seems quite sure of its point of view. *Run, Nigger, Run* sounds like a lynching song, with its mirthless refrain of rasped laughter, *Heh heh heh heh he-he, Ha ha ha ha ha-ha*, but is he trying to do a black accent, and does the spoken introduction (it's been read as an apology for using the word *Nigger*) imply that he thinks of it as a black song? It's a standard, traceable to the 1820s, and survived a hundred and fifty years as a test piece in banjo-picking contests, variously disguised as *Run, Johnny, Run; Run, Smoke, Run; Run, Boy, Run; Run, Preacher, Run; Run, Rabbit, Run*, but everyone knew what was meant. The chorus, *Run, nigger, run, the patter-roller'll catch you, run, nigger, run, it's almost day*, has been lifted from an older song, possibly of black origin. That the body of Macon's song is about tending the land, and how crop yields change from year to year, makes for a worrying inversion of the pastoral refrain: a world is implied where the cycles of nature are facts less fundamental than that black people run from the patroller. The limited frequency-response makes the banjo sound toy-like (cylinder recordings of the xylophone from the 1890s sound more electronic than a theremin), the picking of each string experienced as one in a cascade of temporary overcomings of resistance, as though a hollow, spherical die, each face weighted, were juddering randomly to a stop. In the cover photo, taken twenty years after this song was recorded, Macon is leaning back in his chair, legs spread, the banjo resting on his belly, the sound as I listen now plucked from the entrails of the one belly in earshot, mine, and familiar, the voice merging with that sound, a crack spreading down and out of the vent from the false vocal folds, a man born a hundred years before me speaking clearly from the deep racism of a 1970s childhood.

Saut Crapaud

Saut Crapaud was recorded by Columbus Fruge (probably Frugé, judging by the name of several modern Cajun musicians) in Memphis, Tennessee on the 18th September 1929. The song plays for one hundred and sixty-nine seconds, of which only seventeen are taken up with vocals. I once asked for the lyrics on a folk music discussion board, and was given these:

Saut crapaud ta queue va bruler
Prends courage a'va repousser
C'est Jacques Petrin pas rien sur la tete
En revenant du Lac Charles en mangeant des bananes

with the translation

Jump toad your tail will burn
Take courage it'll grow back
It's Jacques Petrin with no hat on
Coming back from Lake Charles eating bananas.

The first two lines are certainly what Frugé starts off by singing, but the second two aren't and I can't make out the rest of the words at all. My correspondent is either quoting the words of a different version of the (traditional) song, or is making fun of me. His lyrics are the only ones to be found on the internet and have since spread to other sites. Frugé accompanies himself on the accordion, or rather the accordion plays whenever he isn't singing. The only accompaniment which doesn't let up is Frugé's foot kicking or tapping on a board, with a pressure so variable as to suggest at one point a hand counting off rosary beads for each iteration of the simple, up-beat tune, at another a heart struggling in alcohol withdrawal, the whole organ's power expended, each time, on slamming the valve shut (and don't even think about climbing the stairs). The song opens with thirty-seven seconds of accordion, followed by the first two lines of the lyric. There follows seventeen seconds of accordion, followed by two small fragments of lyric, shouts almost, each a second long and spaced eight seconds apart. Then comes twenty-six seconds of accordion, followed by two five-second bursts of song, spaced forty seconds apart, the first of which repeats the first line of the lyric. The song ends with twenty-four seconds of accordion and an instrumental flourish. It would barely count as a vocal track at all, were it not for the almost literally riveting quality of the voice: it's impossible to concentrate on the accordion, which takes up nine tenths of the track time, because the listener is always either recovering from what the voice has just done or anticipating its return, at irregular and quite unpredictable intervals. I'm told the voice is off-key – it's tempting to think Frugé sings unaccompanied in order to sound less so – but I barely hear it in relation to the accordion at all, except in so far as the accordion allows it its place, a euphoric groaned rasp that will out. The kicked percussion takes the listener's part in the process, sounding at greatest stress just before each burst of vocal, as the pressure mounts to express, and just after, in frustration at having had so little time, each time, in which to express. I think of Columbus Frugé's voice dead in another Memphis, awakening in the Tuat, which I will here call Amenti, paralysed, blind and deaf, helpless in the regions of "the great god who carrieth away souls, who eateth hearts, who feedeth upon offal, who dwelleth in the darkness", having only the one hour of night when the sun-boat traverses his part of Amenti in which to eat, and drink, find food, fight and locate immortality, with the aid of so inadequate a guidebook as I can imagine the voice of Columbus Frugé to have been provided with, re-entering paralysis till a next time which always has almost no hope of happening, accordion barely a shadow of the massed forces of the second death.

Depressions Gone From Me Blues

My friend, American, head inside a fist
-sized rag, tied at the chin, I can't
look, fibres sorted by differential
absorption of blood, has a family and is loved,
is loveable. Fearing taint of the germ
blown out through sinuses and eyes
everybody wants to fuck America now,

a horrid survival and not uncommon.
Is it the guaranteed income, freaks
don't lose their looks, and can the head
think in a smaller pool? Hold water in the mouth
and fire at the chin: born and brought up in a briar
patch, my friend got by on a film of cortex
lining the skull, now imploded but readable still.

The orifice the body corporate
expels him through chosen by lottery
is tonight the one loophole in plain sight
endlessly shrunk from the touch
of these fingers that make do for eyes
and he is only a parrot, given bird flu
in quarantine, changing the status of no land. Blind

Willie McTell carried a gun and navigated by sonar.

For Kylie Minogue and Marianne Faithfull

1.

Rogue atoms on the golden leaf
sentence the structure;
the whole surface, written to
by an ant's gesture

chastens itself
into a clean thing, taken
for the fire-source
by a male wanton babe.

2.

What living earth went in or costed fighting
to constipate this era known by sight reading
you won't drop this again in decades mother
the sucker lit an antique Camel Light

an information blackout on a Honda
divested in a stake-out of a rug
reforms the warp, the woof, the lees:
I'll send you a jug in the morning.

Familiars
for Maggie Graham

in the nowhere unrecognised as such at the top right
the brain does not patch over, not the blind spot
no cat ever leaped out of, bordered by what you know
or that second learned at the centre of night vision

is a holding cell where everything permitted and more
bleeds, called by the pulse at the scar boundary
names you would wish on no-one. Eskimos
build in the ischaemic loss, where it is warmer

out than in. Give them that, Greenland
looks big on a map. Literally nothing doing
where once what you see gently gave out
a shock in itself to halt speech and flash

the return of halting on all possible moves.
Your mother wouldn't teach you to knit
but someone did, part of the head an amulet
too keen to wait to be written, barely

a kitten on the keys, it is trying to help.
We bury the dead or else would extend empathy
without prejudice to the inanimate.
Shot down in giving up, your ghost

does just what ghosts do, won't be told
you didn't die. Knit it a woollen hat.
It blocks a high road into the beloved
who would be stateless, but for it.

Two lychee seedlings

One arose shaped by unforeseen checks
the odd leaf curled by red spider I never see
in this dry house flee from a simple dusting of water
the first adult pair irrecoverably scorched
the topmost leaflet fallen, petiole still green
above the unrolling copper threatened by silk
at the growing point.

One is as yet a root,
it has lifted the stone half-clear of earth
the shoot grown into itself in the fork of the loop
sent down from retained seed-leaves
by repeated false starts is slowed to a red wooden knot
still green and white at the base
where side roots make light
of each broken tip.

i.m. Ralph J. Mills, Jr.

About the Author

Peter Manson was born in Glasgow, Scotland in 1969. His books and pamphlets include *me generation* (Writers Forum, 1997), *Adjunct: an Undigest* (Edinburgh Review, 2005), *Before and After Mallarmé* (Survivors' Press, 2005) and *For the Good of Liars* (Barque Press, 2006). An audio CD of extracts from *Adjunct: an Undigest* was released by Stem Recordings in 2004. He co-edits the Object Permanence pamphlet series with Robin Purves, and was the 2005-06 Judith E. Wilson Visiting Fellow in Poetry at the University of Cambridge. His website, *Freebase Accordion*, is at www.petermanson.com.